Also by James McDermott

Manatomy (Burning Eye Books, 2020)

Erased (Polari Press, 2021)

GREEN APPLE RED

James McDermott

ISBN: 978-1-915079-40-4

Cover designed by Aaron Kent

Edited and typeset by Aaron Kent

Broken Sleep Books Ltd
Rhydwen,
Talgarreg,
SA44 4HB
Wales

Contents

Green Apple Red

James McDermott

This pamphlet is dedicated to the memory of my father Shaun McDermott who died aged sixty from COVID-19 on 28th January 2022 during the editing of this publication. Thank you for teaching me to read and write.

Stallion

trudging through autumn fields   I find
a lone pony   bag on its mouth

and I'm thirteen again
in the farmyard of the school changing rooms

a tall muscly stallion
kicks me to bleached tiles   I land on all fours

he forces my head into his sports bag
to sniff his salt sweet shorts

he snorts   stamps   brays   trots off
to the showers   I hear the slam

of locker doors and picture prisons   but
it's a gate being closed

in this field   I wander on   thinking about that
animal   praying he has been put down

The Weight

you call me out as fruit because I am

a lad with pink lady atop my head

to be tiny target   I eat nothing

but granny smiths   you mark me

light in the loafers   to become light

I eat only cox's   medium sized

apples are eighty calories   russets

are fat free   you teach me homo

in tongue of reduction

I juice myself   turn myself to cider

flammable   you brand me faggot which

means kindling   I learn to burn   my body

disappears when you say poof

Intestines

the total surface area of your intestines
is about half the size of a badminton court
September 3rd 2005 ten past twelve period four
I spew my guts on the school sports hall floor
my intestines are athletic
they move food with a wave-like pattern
of muscular actions   peristalsis
I know what I want derives from the Greek
my thoughts   long hollowed coiled tubes
that lead to the anus   fit boys
call me faggot   a type of food
the intestines absorb the nutrients
then force out waste into the rectum
where nerves create sensations that make you
feel like a shit   but I cannot pass
it gathers in the stomach   my second brain
it makes me bottom heavy   shuttlecock
it piles until it fills my liver   heart
lungs   oesophagus   oral cavity
it makes me sick
humans breathe about twenty five thousand times a day
humans are the only animal to blush

Shame's Stone

ages five to twenty six   when a boy
stares smirks smiles kisses my face
flushes as blood rushes   pushes my shame
to the surface a stone   at the centre of my
cherry   tart flesh surrounds a pit with a kernel inside
the drilling worm that turns green apple red
I'm five a day   cricket ball small
shame rises   bobs on my body of
water   it unfolds like
a note passed around class   is my shame like
that boy from school   who passed that note around
who I didn't like then and don't like now
is my shame like the first boy I
dated   who made me hard   who sucked me dry
who shoved me to the side of my life   who
made me put pen to paper   to write him
sonnets   does my shame feel like
nineties comics   Judge Dread   Dandy
from my childhood   juxtaposed images
actions   snatches of dialogue   something
I hang on to   but mean to throw away
a comic book baddy   nobody
can destroy The Joker   hell bent
on taking me hostage   taking over
the city of my mind   a comic book
super hero   who has a unique view
of themselves   the universe   who
can turn shame's poison into petrol
into medicine   into poetry   all

these shamed selves live in me like annual rings
in sweet chestnut   I can't remember
who first threw shame's stone in the sea of me
but I remember each ripple

A Man's Best Friend

ambling alone   I see the pit bull roll
onto his back then his handsome owner
tickles his belly   coos I love you boy

to be that hound   to demand   to receive
that kind of affection   to be loved by
a man   shamelessly   publicly   how come

we train one another to stop loving
flagrantly   openly   like animals
because we are   is this why dogs are men's

best friends   having a pooch allows blokes to
express feelings without being told to
man up   express blatant honest love for

their boy   who they come home to   sweet talk
cook for   watch TV with   then take to bed

We're Animals

we're cubs
we're otters
we're up each other like rats up drain pipes
we take the bull by the horn
we're the worm that turned
we're the pink sheep of the family
we're a wolf in our Mum's clothing
we're a bee in Gran's bonnet
we're elephants in the room
we're flies on the wall
we're sitting ducks
we're scapegoats

My Queer Mind Goes For A Walk

when I stroll through Norfolk woodland
bluebells   blackberries   Golden Wonder
cheese and onion crisp packets   my body
passes other walkers on the straight path
my epidermis feels their peepers burn
questions into my flesh   as if I am
prey   predator   is that a queer body
among brambles   ivy   a broken bike
why does he mince through our woodland   is it
to cruise for sex
the sly foxes are at it like rabbits
in the dog rose   cow parsley   fag packets
I am here to wander   to exercise
to smell wet sedge   to hear jays sing   to spy
muntjacs   badgers   squirrels   weasels   hedgehogs
who see me   as just another animal

Bears

there are several types of bear   Asian
Black   American Black   Brown   adult males

have large bodies   stocky legs   small rounded
ears   shaggy hair   big paws   for bears   staring

is an aggressive act   bears snort   moan   blow
tongue click   jaw click   lip pop   bears claw   bears bite

bears rub themselves up against trees to leave
their scent   to mark territory   bears like

to dominate   bears love fresh meat   bears feast
on anything   bears are hunted   their flesh

their fur   in sub cultures   bears are worshipped
bears are seen as father figures   bears are

sometimes made to bop for entertainment
bears   cubs   don't just live in forests   Google

defines bear as mammal   toy   to carry
a weight   to be rugged shaggy man's man

Outsiders

behind bushes of ripe leaves
drooping like limp wrists
I enter the warrens of dark
dripping meandering corridors
to a place between places   a nowhere
an everywhere   an other world inside
this world   a wild life within the wildlife
where we fallen fruit trees   all uprooted
bearing our rings   create a club within
the scrub   I kneel in front of him   his fly
cracks open like a chrysalis
then the slow unrolling
I plant my mouth
inhale   exhale   my breath
passes through his body of water
until we become a shower
of dandelion seeds   we wish
to reclaim our nature
to be out in the open
to be outsiders
to be easy outside in our bodies

Inosculation

inosculation is
a natural phenomenon

in which the trunks   branches   roots of two trees
grow together

it's most common
with trees of the same kind

the branches first grow separately
in proximity to each other until

they touch
then bark

abrades away
as the trees blow in the wind

they self-graft   they grow together   expand
ambling alone through High Kelling woodland

I clock tree carved cave art   your names in hearts
GS   GG   1997

were you two boys   both penknife sharp
who met in this woodland just to explore

did you find shelter in each other
did your trunk's inosculate

limbs bending around one another
I kiss your names   I hug your hearts

Queen

alone during COVID 19 lock down
I trudge away the days through Runton woods

dreaming the ten watt sun to be pink strobe
thick fog to be dry ice   hot breath   raindrops

to be glitter   wet ground to be sticky
with sweat   spilt shots   longing to find a mate

then I hear him   a bee   fizzing with want
male bees are drones who live to mate with queens

I see him   in yellow black fur   waspish
I watch him buzz round heather   rosemary

bees communicate by waggle dancing
to show other bees where the nectar is

part of a colony   but not right now
happy   drinking in the natural world

smell spilt Jack Daniels   Tennessee honey
the fog becomes dry ice   the sun a strobe

Wild Flowers

Hoary Plantain   Corky Fruited Dropwort
Purple Loosestrife   Night Flowering Catchfly
you plants in the wrong place   I pick you up

unwanted in nature's man made spaces
farm fields   backyards   public parks
I want you   I take you in my basket

how are your shades of green deemed unsightly
Mantis   Crocodile   Islamic   Jungle
Neon   Hooker's   I press you between hard covers

I don't label you weeds   I name you
Hedge Bedstraw   Oxeye Daisy   Corncockle
Bladder Campion   Forget Me Not   Vetch

I preserve you   you wild flowers who thrive
in nature where you survive all seasons
each bud punching through mud to unclench tiny fists

to bloom eternally   long after man
who said you don't belong   *Tansy Scented Mayweed*
Cocksfoot   Timothy Upright   Shepherd's Purse

Gardening

in Sheringham   I have a small cottage
garden that spills onto the shingle beach

the only wall that borders it is horizon
I plant pansies   tie dyed roses

green carnations   violets
rainbow wall flowers

I want Creeping Charlie to over run
flora   take up space   coalesce   create

new forms   in my Eden   I'm God   Mother
Nature   no one forbidden entry   fruit

How Queer I Live On Norfolk Coast

a sudden gust turns the reed bed
to whispering sea
the wind blows me
to wander lonely as a queer

to see all these trunks   thick to the touch
their exposed skins glistening
I belly slide along muscular arms
become bird   lizard   caterpillar   crepuscular squirrel

to gaze down on village people
tourists cruising   daddies hammering pegs
erect tents to camp   out in the sticks
duckies   otters

foxes   flies   free ranging cocks
bushes   cottages   pansies   dirt tracks   dykes
everything always opening
everything always coming out

Acknowledgements

Thanks to the editors of the following magazines and journals where these poems, or earlier versions of them, first appeared: *Anthropocene* ('Gardening'), *Atrium* ('Stallion'), *Cephalo Press* ('The Weight' and 'Bears'), *Finished Creatures* ('Inosculation' and 'Wild Flowers'), *Fourteen Poems* ('Shame's Stone'), *Lunate* ('We're Animals'), *Shooter* ('Queen'), *Stanchion* ('A Man's Best Friend') and *You Are Here: The Queer Ecologies Journal of Creative Geography* ('My Queer Mind Goes For A Walk' and 'How Queer I Live On Norfolk Coast').

'Intestines' was Commended in The York Poetry Prize 2021 judged by Kim Moore.

'Shame's Stone' is written after Richard Scott.

'My Queer Mind Goes For A Walk' is written after Jason Allen-Paisant.

'How Queer I Live On Norfolk Coast' is written after Arielle Greenberg

Lines 1-13 of Inosculation are adapted from Wikipedia's article on inosculation.

Early drafts of several of these poems were workshopped in Anthony Anaxagorou's Advanced Poetry Workshop and Remi Graves' Writing Queer Sex Course, both facilitated by Poetry School. My thanks to Anthony & to Remi, to Poetry School and to my fellow writers in these groups for their feedback.

My thanks to Arts Council England for the Developing Your Creative Practice Grant that gave me the space, time and money to research, write and edit this pamphlet with mentoring from Richard Scott.

My thanks to Richard Scott for his time, insight, encouragement, generosity and thorough thoughtful feedback on these poems.

LAY OUT YOUR UNREST

Milton Keynes UK
Ingram Content Group UK Ltd.
UKHW040954050923
428080UK00004B/101